Scott Foresman

Decodable
Readers 13-24
Unit 2

PEARSON
Scott
Foresman

Editorial Offices: Glenview, Illinois • Parsippany, New Jersey
New York, New York
Sales Offices: Needham, Massachusetts • Duluth, Georgia • Glenview,
Illinois • Coppell, Texas • Sacramento, California • Mesa, Arizona

ISBN: 0-328-14501-7

10 V054 14 13 12 11 10 09

Contents

Going Fishing

Written by Sandra Demnik
Illustrated by Dan Vick

Phonics Skill
Digraphs sh, th

with	fish	this	shack
that	them	shut	then

Tad is with his mom
and dad at the pond.

Tad has his rod.
"I can get many fish with this."

Dad stops at the shack.
"Dad is renting that one," Mom said.

Dad and Mom get fish.
"Put them into this. Shut the lid."

Tad is sad.
Mom has fish.
Dad has fish.

Then Tad tugs and tugs.
It is big!

Tad tugs and then plop!
This is not a fish!

Get the Ball

Written by Christina Potter
Illustrated by Bonnie Smith

Phonics Skill
Sound of a in ball, walk

| ball | small | call | walk | talk | tall |

Hit the ball, Ben.
Ben can not hit it.

Hit the ball, Nick.
Nick hits the ball.

It is in that tree.

Ben and Nick are small.
They can not get it.

Call Tim.
Can Tim get the ball?
Tim can not get the ball.

Walk up and talk to Mom.
Mom is tall.

Mom can get the ball.
Hit the ball, Mom.

Wake Up, Nate

Written by Mary Brown
Illustrated by Joseph Thompson

Phonics Skill
Long a (CVCe)

wake	Nate	late	make	lake	shade
game	gate	skate	bake	cake	plate

Wake up, Nate! Wake up!
It is late.

TickTock TickTock TickTock TickTock

Nate will wake up.
Nate will make his bed.

TickTock TickTock TickTock TickTock

Nate will swim in the lake
and rest in the shade.

TickTock TickTock TickTock TickTock

Nate will catch a ball and
help win the game.

TickTock TickTock TickTock TickTock

Nate will shut the gate and
skate on this path.

Nate will bake a good cake
and put it on a plate.

TickTock TickTock TickTock TickTock

Nate will do all this.
But Nate must wake up.
Wake up, Nate! Wake up!

24

Where Is Dave?

Written by John Parquette
Illustrated by Nina Bear

Phonics Skills
Cc /s/ and Gg /j/

race   lace   place   face   cage

Dave is not in his cage.
Where is Dave?

Is Dave on the steps?
Did Dave race up the walk?

Did Dave take my ball?
Where is it?

28

Is Dave in bed?
Did Dave get this sock?

This had a lace.
Where did it go?

Is Dave in this place?
Is that his face?

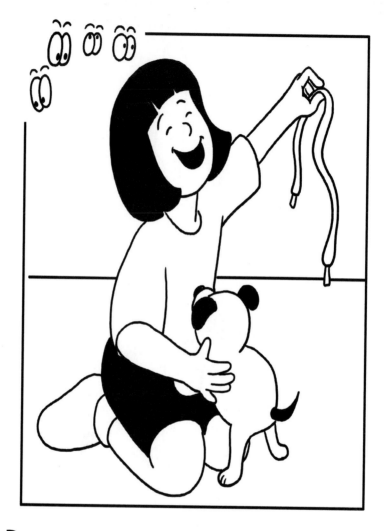

Dave jumps up.
Yes, Dave is here!

A Home for Cat

Written by Ron Holmes
Illustrated by Kris Gosler

Phonics Skill

Long i (CVCe)

bike	hide	fine	time	ride
line	like	mine	Mike	smile

Pat is on his bike.
Dad is with him.

A small cat can hide in the box.
But Pat can see it.

It is a fine cat.
"Can it come with us?" Pat asks.

It is time to go.

Pat and Dad ride to the
shop and get in line.
Cats like this!

"Mom, this cat is mine."

"Can we name it Mike?" Pat asks.
"Mike it is!"
Mom and Dad smile.

Bus Ride

Written by Mary Brenton
Illustrated by Lee Moore

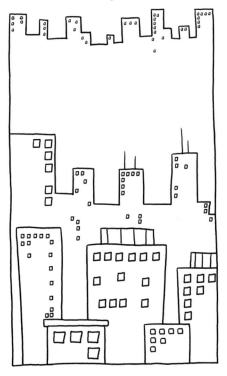

Phonics Skill

Digraphs wh, ch, -tch

which	catch	white	such
when	pitch	chips	check

Mom and Pam walk to the bus stop.

Which bus can Mom and Pam catch?

Mom and Pam get in line
and then ride the bus.

"Can I get this red and white cap?
It is such a nice fit.
I can put it on when I pitch."

Pam has chips.
Mom gets the check.

When will Mom and Pam go back?

It is time to catch the bus.

Nuts for the Cake

Written by Seline Baxter
Illustrated by Lisa Wells

Phonics Skill

Long o (CVCe)

note	Rose	hope	stove
those	bone	rope	home

Mom is mixing a cake.
"I must get nuts."

"Kate, take this note to Rose.
I hope Rose has nuts."

Rose is working at her stove.
"Take those nuts, Kate, and
put them in this sack."
Rose hands Max a bone.

Jan is jumping rope.
"Can I jump?" asks Kate.

"I must go home."
"Where is that sack?" Jan asks.

"Here it is. Max has it."

"Mom, Rose gave us nuts and a bone."

A Ride to the Lake

Written by Hanna Fross
Illustrated by Martin Hull

Phonics Skill

Contractions n't, 'm, 'll

didn't   isn't   I'm   it'll

Tom rides bikes with Mike and Dad.
Mike and Dad ride up the hill.

Tom didn't want to ride up it.

Dad calls Tom.
"It isn't a big hill."

"Ride up it, Tom," calls Dad.
"I'm going as fast as I can."

"That path has rocks on it."
"It isn't a safe place to ride."

"We can walk back. It'll be fine."

"I'm glad we came," Tom smiles.
"This is fun."

June and Mule

Written by Fran Jacobs
Illustrated by Wanda Stern

Phonics Skills

Long u (CVCe)		Long e (CVCe)
June	Mule	these
huge	rude	
use		

Here is June.
June is small.
June has to go home.

Here is Mule.
Mule is huge.
Mule can help June.

June can ride on Mule
to get there.

But Mule is
rude to June.
It makes June sad.

Mule gave June these.
June will not be sad.

Mule takes June to Frog.
Can Frog ride too?

Frog hops on Mule.
June and Frog use Mule
to get home.

Luke Meets Duke

Written by Elizabeth Hawkins
Illustrated by Carl Alderman

Phonics Skill

Inflected Ending -ed

asked   looked   added   called   walked

Luke sat at his home
on a dune.

June came with a cute mule.
Luke asked his name.

"His name is Duke," June said.
"Duke is a fine mule."

Duke looked at Luke.
"Duke likes Luke,"
June added.

"Can Duke eat with
us?" Luke asked.
"It will be fun!"

"Duke!" June called.
Duke walked fast.
Duke looked glad.

"Duke eats cubes,"
June said. She
gave Duke his cubes.

The Seed

Written by Lee Blanton
Illustrated by Dan Vick

Phonics Skill

Long e (ee, e)

Lee	seed	sleep	he	week
green	weed	tree	be	sweet

Lee planted his seed.
"Sleep well, seed,"
Lee said.

He checked his seed.
He gave it water.

In a week, his plant shot up!
It was green.

His mom said,
"That plant grows fast.
Is it a weed?"

"It is a tree,"
Lee said with pride.
"It will be big."

It did grow big.
It gave good shade.

"That seed made
a fine tree," Lee
said with a sweet smile.

Bandit

Written by Renee Johnson
Illustrated by Barbra Kimble

Phonics Skill

Syllables VCCV

Bandit   kitten   rabbits   basket

Bandit is my pup.
He was three weeks old
when we got him.

Dad and Mom like Bandit.
He is small, but he will be big.

Bandit ran to meet the kitten.
She ran up a tree.

Now she likes Bandit.
They sleep together.

Bandit likes rabbits,
but rabbits do not
like him.

Bandit likes jumping
up on me.
Mom gives Bandit food.

Bandit sleeps
in his black basket.
His bed is soft.